Why Is This Festival Special?

Hanukkah

Jillian Powell

W

FRANKLIN WATTS

LONDON•SYDNEY

This edition 2009

Franklin Watts
338 Euston Road
London NW1 3BH

Franklin Watts Australia
Level 17/207 Kent Street
Sydney NSW 2000

Copyright © Franklin Watts 2005

Series editor: Sarah Peutrill
Art director: Jonathan Hair
Picture researcher: Diana Morris
Design: Ian Thompson
Consultant: Jonathan Gorsky, Council of
Christians and Jews

A CIP catalogue record for this book is available from the
British Library

ISBN: 978 0 7496 9014 4
Dewey Classification: 296.4'35

Printed in Malaysia

Franklin Watts is a division of Hachette Children's Books,
an Hachette UK company.
www.hachette.co.uk

COMHAIRLE CHONTAE ÁTHA CLIATH THEAS
SOUTH DUBLIN COUNTY LIBRARIES

MOBILE LIBRARIES
TO RENEW ANY ITEM TEL: 459 7834
OR ONLINE AT www.southdublinlibraries.ie

Items should be returned on or before the last date below. Fines, as displayed in the Library, will be charged on overdue items.

Contents

A festival of lights

Hanukkah is the Jewish festival of lights.

It celebrates light in the short days of November or December. The festival begins on the 25th day of the Jewish month of Kislev (see page 29), and lasts for eight days.

A Jewish boy wearing a skull cap called a kippah reads from the Torah (also shown below).

Jews follow a religion called Judaism. They try to follow the rules and laws written in their holy book, the Torah. They believe that God taught them these laws through the prophet Moses.

At Hanukkah, Jews remember a time when Jews fought to be free to follow their religion. The lights of Hanukkah stand for the freedom to follow their religion and beliefs.

> *Hanukkah is sometimes close to Christmas time. We have fairy lights and decorations and we give presents like people do at Christmas.*
>
> Rebecca, aged 9

Hanukkah is a time for Jewish families to be together at home.

The Hanukkah story

At Hanukkah, Jews celebrate a miracle that saved the Holy Temple of Jerusalem.

They remember a time over 2,000 years ago, when the Syrian-Greeks ruled in Judea, which is now part of Israel.

The King of the Syrian-Greeks, Antiochus IV, attacked the Holy Temple in Jerusalem and stopped Jews worshipping there.

An old picture of the walled city of Jerusalem.

Israel is in a region called the Middle East in Asia.

EUROPE

MIDDLE EAST

Israel

AFRICA

But in 164 BCE, in a town called Modin, the Jews began to fight back. They freed Jerusalem and the Holy Temple, and began to clean it and get it ready for Jews to worship there again.

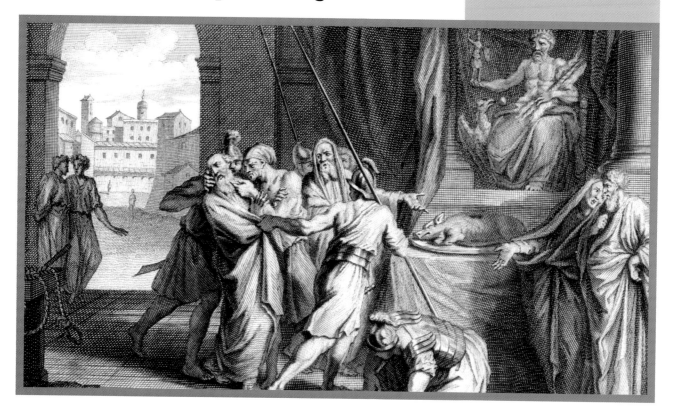

It was important to light the golden menorah (a kind of lamp) in the Temple, but there was only enough oil to last one day. The Jews knew it would take eight days to get more. But the oil kept the lamp burning for eight days.

This is the miracle that Jews celebrate at Hanukkah.

66 We did a play at school about finding the oil in the Temple, and how it kept burning, so Jews could worship again. 99

Daniel, aged 10

The hanukiah

Jews remember the miracle in the Temple by lighting candles.

Jewish school children light candles in a hanukiah in their classroom.

Each day, in homes and in synagogues, Jews light one candle in a hanukiah. This is a candlestick that can hold nine candles. They use one candle to light one more candle each day after sunset, until all the candles are lit at the end of the festival.

The hanukiah has nine candle holders. There are eight candles, one for each night of Hanukkah. The ninth candle, called the Shamash, is used to light the others.

The hanukiah is put by a window or door so that everyone can see the lights burning. The lights must not be used for anything, except to remind people of the Hanukkah miracle. Sometimes, everyone in a family has their own hanukiah.

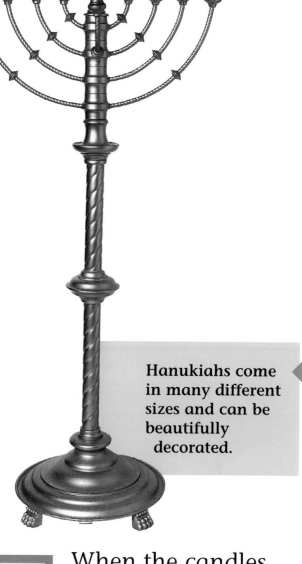

" My sister and I each have our own hanukiah. It's a special part of the day when we light the candles. "

Naomi, aged 10

Hanukiahs come in many different sizes and can be beautifully decorated.

When the candles are lit, families spend time teaching children about Hanukkah, or enjoying songs and games together.

A giant hanukiah in a park in Connecticut, USA.

11

Prayers, songs and blessings

Hanukkah is celebrated with prayers, songs and blessings.

There are services in synagogues every morning of the festival. There are readings from the Torah, songs and prayers including a special prayer for Hanukkah called 'al hanissim'.

> " *I was asked to light the candles in the hanukiah in our synagogue last year.* "
> Nathan, aged 10

These boys are praying in their synagogue.

After prayers, everyone sings the group of psalms called the Hallel. This is when the candles in the hanukiah are lit, often by children.

At home, Jews sing blessings and prayers as they light the candles in the hanukiah. They sing three blessings on the first night, and two on the other nights of the festival.

Children singing psalms at a Hanukkah service. They each wear a prayer shawl (tallit).

Children also sing songs about Hanukkah at school.

Children sing about the number of candles on a hanukiah.

Games

Families like to have fun and play games together at Hanukkah.

The dreidel game is a popular game of chance. A dreidel is a spinning top that has a Hebrew letter on each of its four sides.

" We play the dreidel game when we visit my grandma. It's a lot of fun. "
David, aged 8

Each player takes a turn to spin their dreidel.

There is a story that the dreidel game began when the Jews were stopped from reading their holy book, the Torah, by the Syrian-Greeks. Jewish people got together secretly to study the Torah, but when a Syrian-Greek soldier went past, they took out their dreidels and pretended to play.

Dreidels are made from different materials like wood, china or plastic and in all sorts of colours.

Children may also play board games or do special craft projects or puzzles at Hanukkah. These are often decorated with Hanukkah candles and dreidels.

Pictures made with sand and a children's jigsaw decorated with the symbols of Hanukkah.

15

Cards and gifts

Jewish families exchange cards and gifts to wish each other Happy Hanukkah.

We made cards for Hanukkah in my class. I stuck candle shapes on mine.

Tom, aged 9

HAPPY HANUKKAH

Sometimes, children make their own Hanukkah cards at home or in school. They may decorate them with hanukiahs or dreidels.

Hanukkah cards made from coloured paper and decorated with a hanukiah and dreidel.

Happy Hanukkah

Children may be given presents in grab bags. These contain surprise gifts such as sweets and small toys or games. Hanukkah gifts are always small treats, because this is a religious festival, and not just about food or presents.

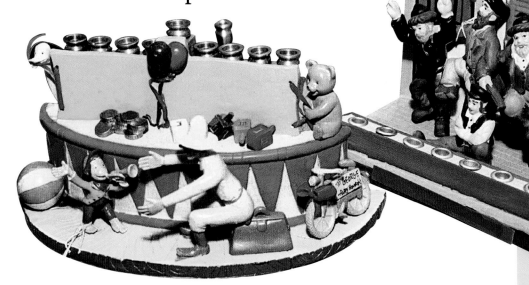

Some families like to give small gifts on each of the eight nights of the festival. It is traditional for parents and grandparents to give children yellow bags of real or chocolate money. This is called gelt.

Colourful hanukiahs designed as gifts for children.

Children may receive chocolate coins wrapped in gold paper.

Decorations

Decorations are important at Hanukkah.

In Israel and in Jewish communities around the world, people put up decorations outside.

> **"** *I like helping to put up the decorations for Hanukkah. Dad puts fairy lights at the front of the house.* **"**
> Nathan, aged 10

A giant hanukiah and fairy lights decorate a street in Israel.

Many Jewish families decorate inside their homes for the festival, too. They put out hanukiahs and sometimes hang fairy lights.

Jews also hang banners, and paper decorations showing hanukiahs, candles, dreidels and the Star of David.

Decorative dreidels hanging in a Jewish home.

A six-pointed Star of David is a Jewish symbol throughout the world.

The traditional colours for Hanukkah are blue and white, the colour of the sky or heavens. This reminds people that the miracle of Hanukkah comes from God.

19

Festive food

Many foods eaten at Hanukkah are fried in oil, to remind people of the miracle of the Temple lamp.

In Israel, and other parts of the Middle East, north Africa and southern Europe, Jewish families eat fried doughnuts called sufganiyot.

The doughnuts have jam inside.

Cheese and other dairy foods are eaten in many Hanukkah dishes.

Cheese is another traditional food for Hanukkah. It reminds Jews of the story of Judith, who helped the Jews fight against the Syrian-Greeks. She fed the Syrian-Greek General salty cheese. This made him so thirsty that he drank a lot of wine and became drunk, so Judith was able to cut off his head!

Savoury latkes fried in oil.

Jews from eastern Europe cook latkes, which are pancakes made with eggs and potatoes. They eat them with onions and vegetables or as a sweet, with honey and spices.

This tradition has spread to other parts of the world, such as the USA.

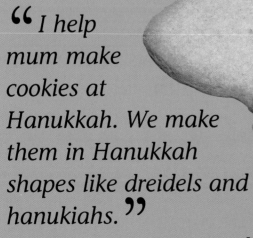

" I help mum make cookies at Hanukkah. We make them in Hanukkah shapes like dreidels and hanukiahs. "

Jess, aged 9

21

Hanukkah holiday

In Israel, everyone has a holiday at Hanukkah.

There are lots of special events when people get together to light hanukiahs or go to dinners, parties and concerts. Some towns and cities have a funfair for the children and a craft fair with festive food and presents for sale.

> **"** *I look forward to Hanukkah because we get a whole week off school!* **"**
>
> Alex, aged 10

A colourful street procession in Israel. This is part of the Three Holidays Festival, which celebrates Christmas, Hanukkah and Ramadan.

Schools close for a whole week so children can celebrate the festival. Sometimes they put on plays for parents and friends.

School children hold lamps as they act out the story of Hanukkah.

Important buildings, like the Israeli Parliament House, are decorated with giant hanukiahs lit up with electric lights.

The City Hall in Tel Aviv, Israel, lit up as a giant hanukiah.

Torch relay

Hanukkah is celebrated each year with torch relays.

On the eve of Hanukkah, marathon runners go to the town of Modin in Israel. They light torches and then carry them all the way to the Western Wall in Jerusalem. This is the last wall left standing from the Holy Temple of Jerusalem.

A runner brings a torch to the holy site of the Western Wall in Jerusalem as the evening light fades.

Nine flames burn in the hanukiah at the Western Wall.

The last runner hands his torch to the chief rabbi who lights the first candle of a giant hanukiah.

Young Jewish people also take part in torch relays in the USA, and other countries. They carry torches to celebrate Hanukkah, and to bring together Jews living in different parts of the world.

" Last year, we had a torch relay in our city. There was quite a crowd watching the runners who had come over from Israel to celebrate Hanukkah with us. "

Michael, aged 10

Sharing and giving

Hanukkah is a time for giving to charity and thinking of others.

Many Jewish families like to give to charity at Hanukkah. This is called tzedekah. Children join in, sometimes giving a toy or some of their pocket money.

When the hanukiah is lit, many families sit down together. They remember the miracle of Hanukkah and what it means.

The festival is a time for giving thanks to God for helping the Jews. It is also a time for helping others, and thinking about those who are poor, sick or in need.

Family is very important to Jews. Hanukkah is a time to remember families in need.

❝ *Mum and Dad put an extra present in our Hanukkah grab bags for us to give to help children in need.* **❞**

Rebecca, aged 8

27

Glossary

Dreidel a spinning top that can be filled with sweets or money.

Grab bags party bags containing surprise gifts and sweets.

Hanukiah a candlestick that holds nine candles, lit for Hanukkah.

Hebrew the language of the Jewish people. It is the main language spoken in Israel.

Latkes potato pancakes that are fried in oil.

Miracle an amazing event that people believe God made happen.

Moses one of the first leaders of the Jews. He led them out of Egypt where they were slaves, to be a free people.

Prophet a teacher who tells people how God wants them to live.

Rabbi a Jewish religious teacher.

Shamash the candle used to light the other eight candles in a hanukiah.

Star of David a star with six points, that is used as a Jewish symbol.

Synagogue a building where Jews go to worship and study.

Torah the most important Jewish holy book.

Torch relay when a torch is carried and passed from one runner to another.

Tzedekah money given by Jews to help the poor.

Judaism

Judaism is one of the oldest religions in the world. There are about 12 million Jews around the world, mostly living in Israel, a Jewish state, or in the USA. Some people are Jewish but do not actively practise Judaism.

Religious Jews believe there is one God, who created everything in the universe. They believe that God chose the Jews as His people. He taught them His rules and laws through the prophet Moses. He gave them these rules to obey and in return He promised to look after them.

Jews worship God with ceremonies, prayers and blessings, and by reading their holy books, especially the Torah.

Home and family life are very important to Jews. They celebrate several religious festivals each year that remember times in their history:

Passover recalls the time when the Jews escaped from captivity in Egypt.

Shavuot reminds Jews of the time when Moses received God's laws on Mount Sinai.

Sukkot recalls the time that the Jews spent in the desert on their way to the Promised Land.

All these festivals take their dates each year from the Jewish calendar, which is based on the sun and the moon. The Jewish month of Kislev, which Hanukkah falls in, is in November or December in a Western calendar.

Index